In the Spotlight

Elon Musk

by Kaitlyn Duling

Bullfrog Books

Ideas for Parents and Teachers

Bullfrog Books let children practice reading informational text at the earliest reading levels. Repetition, familiar words, and photo labels support early readers.

Before Reading

- Discuss the cover photo. What does it tell them?
- Look at the picture glossary together. Read and discuss the words.

Read the Book

- "Walk" through the book and look at the photos. Let the child ask questions. Point out the photo labels.
- Read the book to the child, or have him or her read independently.

After Reading

- Prompt the child to think more. Ask: What did you know about Elon Musk before reading this book? What more would you like to learn about him after reading it?

Bullfrog Books are published by Jump!
5357 Penn Avenue South
Minneapolis, MN 55419
www.jumplibrary.com

Library of Congress Cataloging-in-Publication Data

Names: Duling, Kaitlyn, author.
Title: Elon Musk / by Kaitlyn Duling.
Description: Minneapolis, MN : Jump!, [2019]
Series: In the spotlight
"Bullfrog Books." | Includes index.
Identifiers: LCCN 2018018924 (print)
LCCN 2018019793 (ebook)
ISBN 9781641282000 (e-book)
ISBN 9781641281980 (hardcover : alk. paper)
ISBN 9781641281997 (pbk.)
Subjects: LCSH: Musk, Elon—Juvenile literature.
SpaceX (Firm) —Juvenile literature. | Tesla Motors
Juvenile literature. | Businesspeople—United
States—Biography—Juvenile literature.
Classification: LCC HC102.5.M88 (ebook)
LCC HC102.5.M88 D85 2019 (print) | DDC 338.092 [B]—dc23
LC record available at https://lccn.loc.gov/2018018924

Editor: Susanne Bushman
Designer: Molly Ballanger

Photo Credits: Pascal Le Segretain/Getty, cover; Visual China Group/Getty, 1; Kevork Djansezian/Getty, 3, 8–9, 23br; Ramin Talaie/Getty, 4; John B. Carnett/Getty, 5, 23tr; Joshua Lott/Getty, 6–7; Paul Sakuma/AP Images, 10–11; James Leynse/Getty, 12–13; Fedor Selivanov/Shutterstock, 14, 23tl; benedek/iStock, 15, 22tr; Science Collection/Alamy, 16–17, 23bm; Zuma Press, Inc./Alamy, 17; Federico Rostagno/Shutterstock, 18, 23br; Kyodo News/Getty, 19, 23tm; Brendan Hoffman/Getty, 20–21; Picsfive/Shutterstock, 22tl; Jim Watson/Getty, 22br; Luca Teuchmann/Getty, 24.

Printed in the United States of America at Corporate Graphics in North Mankato, Minnesota.

Table of Contents

Elon

Who is this?
Elon Musk.

He is famous!

Why?

invention

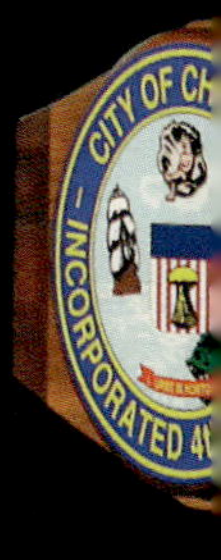

He invents.

He starts companies.
One is now PayPal.
Cool!

Elon Musk
PayPal

TESL

Another one is Tesla.
It makes things.
What? Cars!

They are electric.

Wow!

This is one.

He has many ideas.

Tesla
Model D

SpaceX makes rockets.
They go to space!

He wants to help Earth.

How?

One way is solar panels.

He gives them.

They save energy.

Elon works hard.
His ideas help.
Thanks, Elon!

Key Events

June 28, 1971:
Elon Reeve Musk is born in Pretoria, South Africa.

May 6, 2002:
Elon starts his company SpaceX. The company makes rockets.

July 19, 2006:
Elon unveils the very first Tesla car model, the Roadster.

November 21, 2013:
Fortune magazine names Elon Businessperson of the Year.

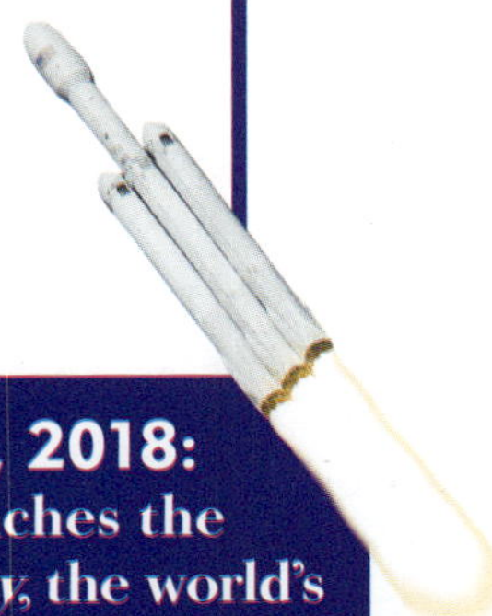

February 6, 2018:
SpaceX launches the *Falcon Heavy*, the world's most powerful rocket at the time.

March 2018:
Forbes magazine lists Elon's net worth at $19.9 billion.

Picture Glossary

electric
Runs off of electricity instead of gasoline.

energy
Power that makes machines work.

famous
Very well-known to many people.

invents
Thinks up and creates new things.

rockets
Vehicles with special engines that can travel fast or far into the air.

solar panels
Devices that absorb sunlight and turn it into electricity.

Index

To Learn More

Finding more information is as easy as 1, 2, 3.

1. Go to www.factsurfer.com
2. Enter "ElonMusk" into the search box.
3. Click the "Surf" button to see a list of websites.